D1490482

POVERTY
IN THE
AMERICAN
DREAM
WOMEN & CHILDREN
FIRST

BY
KARIN STALLARD
BARBARA EHRENREICH
HOLLY SKLAR

STALLARD

POVERTY
IN THE
AMERICAN
DREAM
WOMEN & CHILDREN
FIRST

BY
KARIN STALLARD
BARBARA EHRENREICH
HOLLY SKLAR

SERIES CO-EDITORS:
HOLLY SKLAR & GLORIA JACOBS
DESIGNER: CYNTHIA CARR
TABLES COMPILED BY
KARIN STALLARD & HOLLY SKLAR
WITH JANE BEDELL & RUTHANN EVANOFF

SOUTH END PRESS
1983

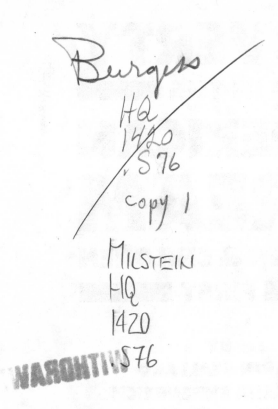
Cover photo: P. Shames

An earlier version of part of this material appeared in *Ms.* magazine as "The Nouveau Poor" (July 1982), written by Barbara Ehrenreich and Karin Stallard with the help of a grant from the Windom Fund.

The table on "Changes in Household Income as a Result of Budget Cuts and Tax Provisions" is reprinted with permission from the Center on Budget and Policy Priorities.

The authors thank the following for their comments on various drafts of this pamphlet: Jane Bedell, Ruthann Evanoff, Ros Everdell, Linda Johnson, Andrea Kydd, Barbara O'Dair, Susan Schechter, and Jon Steinberg.

We especially want to thank all the women whose stories appear throughout this pamphlet.

TABLE OF CONTENTS

LIST OF TABLES & BOXES

CHAPTER 1

WOMEN & CHILDREN FIRST

One morning last summer, Brenda C. woke up crying. "I couldn't take it anymore," she explained. "My welfare check and food stamps were cut and I had to choose between paying the rent or buying food and school clothes for my growing kids—my oldest son's shoe size went from an eight to an eleven over one summer! Things had to be bought. What could I do?"

Cidne Hart/LNS

What Brenda did came as a shock to herself and her two sons, Kenny, 13, and Tony, 8. "I went down and enlisted in the Army," she told us. "It's my last chance to try and support my family. I don't know any other way." Soon after, Brenda left for basic training, leaving Kenny and Tony in the care of a friend until she returned.

Brenda is black, a single parent in her thirties, and like many welfare recipients, she worked whenever she could. Her last job as a VISTA worker, organizing community food and nutrition programs, was eliminated when the Reagan Administration revamped VISTA. The string of low-paid jobs which Brenda held never paid enough to support her family without public assistance. And when she wasn't working, welfare payments alone barely covered rent, household items and school supplies. Often the food stamps didn't last through the end of the month. Brenda and her kids managed by doing without most everything but the essentials. Once their income shrank, however, even the essentials were not affordable.

Avis Parke joined the ranks of the American poor after her divorce from a middle class husband, a minister. Avis, in her early fifties, is white and college educated. Like many other "displaced homemakers," she found a cold greeting in the job market.

Parke vs. Parke was a classic case of a middle-aged man leaving for a younger woman, and when the marriage dissolved so did Avis' middle class lifestyle. Now, Avis and her three youngest children (the oldest three live on their own) have made an unheated, New England summer cottage their year-round home. Avis survives on a tenuous combination of welfare, food stamps, child support and a lot of thriftiness.

Avis and Brenda are among the more than 32 million people who live below the official poverty level: $9,287 for a non-farm family of four in 1981. Today, one out of every seven Americans is poor according to official measures. Many people know that poverty is on the rise. What many do not know is that more and more of the poor are women and their dependent children.

The "Feminization of Poverty"

Two out of three poor adults are women and one out of five children is poor. Women head half of all poor families and over half the children in female-headed households are poor: 50 percent of white children; 68 percent of black and Latin children.[1] A woman over 60 years of age is almost twice as likely as her male counterpart to be impoverished. One-fifth of all elderly women are poor. For elderly black women the poverty rate in 1981 was 43.5 percent; for

Tom Angotti & Belinda Sifford/LNS

elderly Latina women, 27.4 percent. Among black women over 65 living alone the 1982 poverty rate was about 82 percent.[2]

While the "feminization of poverty" isn't yet a household phrase, for growing numbers of women and their dependent children it is an everyday reality. According to sociologist Diana Pearce, who tagged the trend in a 1978 study, 100,000 additional women with children fell below the poverty line each year from 1969 to 1978. In 1979 the number surged to 150,000 and was matched in 1980.[3] Households headed by women—now 15 percent of all households—are the fastest growing type of family in the country.[4]

So clear is the spiraling pattern of women's impoverishment that the President's National Advisory Council on Economic Opportunity observed in September 1981: "All other things being equal, if the proportion of the poor in female-householder families were to continue to increase at the same rate as it did from 1967 to 1978, the poverty population would be composed solely of women and their children before the year 2000."

"All other things," of course, are not equal. Poverty is disproportionately borne by people of color, and with continued racial discrimination and high unemployment there will be many poor men in the year 2000. Yet, however many impoverished men there will be, there will still be many more poor women. Women are increasingly likely to carry primary responsibility for supporting themselves and their children due to rising divorce rates and non-marital childbirths. At the same time, most women remain locked into dead-end jobs with wages too low to support themselves,

Table 1

Poverty
Percent Below Poverty Level 1979-1981

	All Races			White			Black			Latin		
	79	80	81	79	80	81	79	80	81	79	80	81
All Persons	11.7	13.0	14.0	9.0	10.2	11.1	31.0	32.5	34.2	21.8	25.7	26.5
Male	10.1	11.2	12.1	7.8	8.7	9.6	27.3	28.7	29.9	19.0	23.5	24.5
Female	13.3	14.7	15.8	10.3	11.6	12.5	34.1	35.7	37.9	24.4	27.7	28.4
Female Householder*	32.0	33.8	35.2	24.9	27.1	28.4	52.2	53.1	55.8	48.9	52.5	54.0

* Female head of household, with no husband present.

Sources: U.S. Department of Commerce, Bureau of the Census, "Characteristics of the Population Below the Poverty Level," 1979-80, *Current Population Reports*, Consumer Income Series P-60, No. 130 and *Money Income and Poverty Status of Families and Persons in the United States*, 1981.

let alone sustain a family. In 1980 the median income* of a female household head, with no husband present, was $10,408; for black women it was $7,425 and for Latinas, $7,031.

A 1977 government study found that if working women were paid what similarly qualified men earn, the number of poor families would decrease by half.[5] In 1980 the median income of a full-time, year-round working woman was $11,590—versus $19,172 for her male counterpart. In short, there is a fundamental difference between male and female poverty: for men, poverty is often the consequence of unemployment and a job is generally an effective remedy, while female poverty often exists even when a woman works full-time.

Virtually all women are vulnerable—a divorce or widowhood is all it takes to throw many middle class women into poverty. Yet, as Sally Michaels (not her real name), a divorced mother of three, told us, "There is a lot of denial among women. It's like how people are about seat belts. They don't want to wear them because they don't want to face the fact that they're really in danger."

Poverty May Be a Divorce Away

Avis Parke's marriage lasted 30 years, long enough for her to have six children and fulfill all the duties of being a minister's wife. She helped put her husband through school and she moved whenever his career took him to a new parish. They lived comfortably in the parish houses and enjoyed the fringe benefits of a car, health plan and pension fund. Now Avis sells jewelry over the telephone as part of a workfare program which requires her to "work off" her welfare grant. Avis hates being on welfare, but is unable to find a job that pays a living wage and allows her to be home when her children return from school.

Mary Stevens is in a similar situation. In her mid-forties and recently divorced, she made the transition from living in a large house with her husband and son in a New England fishing village to renting a $40-a-week room in a shabby boarding house. Two winters ago she worked in a seasonal federal program—which has since been cut—with more than a dozen other women who call themselves the "nouveau poor" (new poor). "They're all suffering exactly what I

---

*Half of all persons being counted earn incomes below the *median* and half earn incomes above it. Average (or mean) income, on the other hand, tells you what you get when you sum up all the incomes being measured and then divide the total by the number of incomes. For example, the average of 10 incomes which total $200,000 is $20,000. But it could be that one person makes $100,000 while the other nine make $11,111 each.

am," Mary told us. "You want to talk about mad? Everyone of these women is divorced, suffering, no money. We come home with $123 a week. We don't even know how we're going to eat, where the money's coming from, how the kids are going to be fed...You think I'm scared? I go to bed nauseous."

For more and more women poverty begins with divorce. Over one out of three marriages now end in divorce and this usually means financial crisis for the woman and financial gain for the man. A recent California study found that in the first year after a divorce, the standard of living for women plunged by 73 percent while the former husbands experienced a rise in living standard of 42 percent.[6]

Anyone who saw the movie Kramer vs. Kramer is familiar with the woman-in-search-of-fulfillment-leaves-husband-and-child story, with the overworked husband left to pick up the pieces of a broken home. That story is the exception to the rule. Typically, the breakup of a marriage produces a single man and a single mother. Only 2 percent of single parent households are headed by men and most men don't challenge their wives for custody.

Regardless of her ex-spouse's income a woman's chances of subsisting on alimony and child support are pretty slim. Alimony is so scarce that it barely figures into the equation. It is estimated that judges award alimony to only 14 percent of divorcing women and, of those, only 7 percent collect it regularly.[7] (To add insult to injury,

a woman is required to pay taxes on her alimony income while a man deducts alimony payments on his tax return.)

As for child support, the Urban Institute calculated in 1976 that 40 percent of ex-husbands contributed nothing toward their children's support. Of the remaining 60 percent, nearly all paid less than $2,000 a year. In most cases, child support payments drop off sharply after the first three years.[8] The California study found that in 1977 only 13 percent of mothers with pre-school children were awarded any spousal support and only one-third of the divorced mothers sampled received the full amount of child support in the first year following the divorce.

The problem of inadequate or nonexistent child support stems partly from a court system which fails to award and enforce decent sums. It is also rooted in widespread social attitudes which, in effect, condone a divorced father's desertion of his children. "There's a conspiracy of silence about child support," says Diana Pearce. "A man is not afraid to face his colleagues at work if he's cheating on his child support...Cheating on your children is not considered [bad]."

Defaulting on child support cuts across class, race and age lines, just as divorce itself does. "It doesn't matter what [a woman's] previous income was," comments Pearce. "Her chances of getting child support are very small. Middle class men are just as bad, if not worse, than poor men."

Carla was 23 when she picked up her 2 year old daughter and

left her husband, a moderately well-to-do restaurant owner from Long Island. He had a habit of knocking Carla down the stairs and kicking her when she fell. Carla was awarded child support on the condition that her husband have visitation rights with their daughter. But after two of his visits turned into assaults on herself and a third led to the weekend-long kidnapping of her daughter, Carla decided the child support wasn't worth the danger. Now Carla is on welfare and works off the books as a cleaning woman so that she and her child have enough to live on.

The decision to leave a violent husband can be hard enough because of conflicting emotions. But there are tangible stumbling blocks as well. "Many women stay with abusive men and return to them because they have to confront enormous obstacles such as getting housing, relocating their children in new schools, finding jobs—everything," explains Susan Schechter, author of *Women and Male Violence: The Visions and Struggles of the Battered Women's Movement.* Battered women's shelters are too few and often the police and courts are unresponsive. As Schechter puts it, "the message is 'go back home.' " She adds, "In spite of it all, many women do leave, which is a major victory for an incredibly courageous group of survivors."

Displaced Homemakers

In 1977, under pressure from women's organizations and feminist legislators, the New York State Legislature passed a law to provide services for "displaced homemakers." The legislation states the problem this way:

   a. homemakers are an unrecognized and unpaid part of the national workforce who make an invaluable contribution to the welfare and economic stability of the nation but who receive no health, retirement, or unemployment benefits as a result of their labor;

   b. an increasing number of homemakers are displaced in their middle years from their normal family role and left without any source of financial security through divorce, the death of their spouse, or the loss of family income;

   c. displaced homemakers often are subject to discrimination in employment because of age, sex, and lack of any recent paid work experience; and

   d. displaced homemakers often are without any source of income because:

   i. they are ineligible for social security benefits because they are too young, or because they are divorced from the family wage earner;

ii. they are ineligible for federal welfare assistance if they are not physically disabled and their children are past a certain age;

iii. they are ineligible for unemployment insurance because they have been engaged in unpaid labor in the home.[9]

Carol McVicker is program director of WISH (Women In Self Help), a New York State-funded program for displaced homemakers. "The women who come to this program bought the American Dream," she says. "They thought they'd do their part, manage the house, raise the kids, support the husband, perhaps do some volunteer work and, in later years, get some recognition and a secure retirement, maybe even travel. They find out it's not that way—the dream comes crashing down." The term "displaced homemaker" was coined by Tish Sommers, a former California homemaker active in the Cub Scouts and PTA. As Sommers told one reporter, after her divorce at age 57, she realized "[her] identity as a 'career homemaker' no longer fit...[She] was part of an invisible group of previously dependent women who now faced economic discrimination, poverty and humiliation."[10] Sommers formed the

Laurie Leifer/LNS

Income Earning Persons, 1980
14 Years and Older

	All Races		White		Black		Latin	
	Male	Female	Male	Female	Male	Female	Male	Female
Year-round, full-time workers, median income	$19,172	$11,590	$19,719	$11,702	$13,874	$10,914	$13,790	$9,887
All earners, median income	$12,529	$4,919	$13,327	$4,946	$8,008	$4,579	$9,659	$4,405
All earners, percent earning $25,000 & over	17.5	1.9	18.8	2.0	5.8	1.0	7.9	0.7

Source: *Statistical Abstracts*, citing U.S. Bureau of the Census, *Current Population Reports*, Series P-60, No. 127 (August 1981) and unpublished Current Population Survey data.

Table 2

Alliance for Displaced Homemakers and, later, the Older Women's League (OWL) with Laurie Shields, another founding mother of the displaced homemakers movement.

Longtime homemakers find out that housework isn't valued as a job experience, even though, as McVicker points out, housewives hold down many jobs—money manager, childcare worker, cook, nurse, repair person, recreation worker. Still, employers say, "You're not job ready." The paid jobs women may have held before marrying or earlier in the marriage are often low-status, low-paid jobs such as domestic work. The WISH program works on building self-esteem and peer support as well as developing concrete, job-related skills. WISH tries to place women in higher paying jobs with good benefits, or in training and education programs to enhance their skills. But with government cutbacks and high unemployment the entry or reentry of displaced homemakers into the job market is more difficult. The elimination of CETA (Comprehensive Employ-ment Training Administration) has meant more than a loss of training and entry-level jobs for women. Since there is no specific federal legislation for displaced homemakers, some federal funding of programs came through CETA. With its elimination, says McVicker, programs dependent on CETA have been decimated.

At WISH, says McVicker, "we deal with barriers—age barriers, sex barriers, race barriers and education barriers." She adds, "there's no question that it's much harder to get a job if you're not white. You may get the job, but it takes more time, more interviews, more motivation."

Estel Fonseca, vice president for Service Providers of the National Displaced Homemakers Network and former director of the Displaced Homemakers Program of the national Puerto Rican Forum, explains that Latinas face very basic problems of language and isolation. "Many Latinas are not accustomed to dealing with the mainstream culture outside their communities. In our programs we have to overcome lack of English skills and help women learn how to get around by bus and subway and become accustomed to talking with people from different backgrounds."

Then there is the extreme stigma attached to women-headed households. "Within the Latin population, when a woman is divorced or separated, the loss of her man is viewed as being her fault," says Fonseca, "even if the man left her. Latinas have a very hard time accepting their legitimacy as heads of families. Even more than other women, Latinas are socialized to be homemakers and family nurturers. It is very difficult for many women to become the only breadwinner and overcome their feelings of failure and inadequacy."

Moreover, Latinas face severe employment discrimination, having been generally restricted to three job categories: domestic worker, nurse's aide and factory worker (primarily seamstresses in the garment industry). These jobs are among the most underpaid and unprotected by safety and fair employment regulations.

Elderly displaced homemakers run up against the additional barrier of age discrimination. Among the elderly, divorce is overwhelmingly initiated by men, and, as Barbara Cain observes in her article the "Plight of the Gray Divorcee," it hits "a generation of women who had assumed that marriage was a lifetime commitment."

Elderly women are caught in a special financial bind, according to Cain: "Not only will many of them be cut off from their former husbands' private retirement pensions, but they can also be cut off from medical insurance at a time when they may be most vulnerable. Indeed, some divorcees remain perilously unprotected by medical insurance coverage until they reach the age of 64, when they become eligible for Medicare in their own right."[11]

Women with husbands over 62 (the minimum Social Security retirement age) may still fall between the cracks when it comes to Social Security: According to attorney Susan D. Hartman of Michigan, "elderly divorcees solely dependent on their former husbands' Social Security benefits are denied them when their husbands choose not to retire until age 72 (70, after Jan. 1, 1983). And when an ex-husband does retire, the divorcee is entitled to only half of his Social Security benefits, and that...amounts to only a third of the total sum shared as a married couple."[12]

"There's a cultural definition of women as expendable," says Betty Thompson (not her real name), a divorced woman in her fifties. "You are treated like breed cows. And when your term is over—you are over."

CHAPTER 2

WOMEN'S WORK

"Decade of Liberation"
Ironically, the feminization of poverty swung into full gear in the 1970s, the period sometimes called the "decade of liberation" for women. In the media fantasy of the seventies, women sporting skirted suits and sleek attache cases swept into *Fortune* 500 boardrooms and were addressed respectfully as "Ms" and "Chairwoman." Advertising slogans told the contemporary woman

"You've come a long way baby"— and the message was that the only thing holding *any* woman back was a subnormal supply of "assertiveness."

But if the images of women changed, the institutions didn't. While individual women moved up the career ladder, women as a class slid backwards, with those who were doubly discriminated against—women of color—taking the heaviest losses. Today women who work full time earn on the average only 59 cents for every dollar earned by men—*down* from nearly 64 cents in 1955. Black women earn 53 cents and Latinas 49 cents for every dollar earned by men.[13]

Some determined women who had other requirements such as youth and a university education (and perhaps the means to wage a legal battle) did beat a path into previously all-male professions. The number of women lawyers and judges, for example, rose from 4 percent in 1971 to 14 percent a decade later. There were similar increases in medicine, college teaching and middle-level management.[14] In the world of high finance, however, few women entered corporate boardrooms in any capacity besides secretary or cleaning

woman. In 1981 women still accounted for only 2 percent of all corporate directors and 6 percent of all managers.[15]

In blue-collar fields the gains look dramatic at first glance, with the number of women rising by 80 percent in the 1970s. But this increase is so high because women were virtually excluded from these occupations until then. Today, only 3 percent of machinists, 2 percent of electricians and 1 percent of auto mechanics are women. Overall, women now hold 2 percent of all skilled craft jobs compared to 1 percent in 1961.[16]

Even in areas where women did make real steps forward there are reasons to be skeptical. Sally Steenland of the Center for Women and Work (part of the National Commission on Working Women) comments: "There is quite a lot of evidence, both researched and anecdotal, showing that when women enter any job category or profession in droves, that occupation loses status. Men don't want it anymore, and the salaries become lower. It happened to bank tellers in recent years...and it happened a century ago when the male clerk was replaced by the female secretary...[when] a department gets a reputation as a female ghetto [it's] no longer seen as a step on the ladder to the top."[17]

The Pink Collar Ghetto

Female participation in the paid labor force is higher today, at 52 percent of all women, than at any time in history. But a job is not necessarily an antidote to poverty for women. On the contrary, the jobs available to women are part of the problem.

Women "are as occupationally segregated today as they were at

the end of the Victorian era," observes Diana Pearce.[18] The great majority of women workers remain clustered in 20 out of 420 occupations listed by the Bureau of Labor Statistics. These so-called "pink collar" jobs are all too familiar: clerical work, nursing, domestic work, restaurant and food service, retail sales, light assembly, elementary school teaching, etc. Women account for nearly 99 percent of all receptionists and 97 percent of all secretaries and nurses.[19]

"Women's work" is systematically underpaid. In 1981 full-time secretaries averaged $229 a week, practical nurses $227 and cashiers $166. Even when men and women share the same occupation men's earnings outstrip women's. Full-time female clerical workers averaged $9,855 in 1981 while men in similar positions averaged $16,503.[20] On the same floor of a department store you may find a man selling large appliances such as washing machines while a woman sells suitcases. Men don't have a natural ability to sell washing machines and women don't have a natural instinct for luggage, but it's the appliance sale that brings a commission. In 1980 female salespersons averaged $176 a week while men in comparable positions averaged $337.[21] This discriminatory pattern holds true all the way up the income scale. Less than 2 percent of all female workers earn $25,000 or more, compared to 17.5 percent for men.

Women in trade unions do financially better than their unorganized sisters, averaging 73 cents for every dollar earned by union men. *Southern Exposure*, a journal on life in the South, reports that in the South women in trade unions earned an average of $1,456 to $2,652 more in 1977 (depending on the region) than non-union women.[22] But, today only 15 percent of women workers are organized nationwide. The trade union movement has only recently begun to focus on women workers, with women-led organizations such as District 925 of the Service Employees International Union—a joint venture with Working Women, the National Association of Office Workers—and the Coalition of Labor Union Women (CLUW) at the fore.

In recent years, there's been a backlash against affirmative

action as so-called "reverse discrimination." The fact is that women college graduates earn about as much as a man with an eighth grade education.[23] Clearly discrimination is real, and it remains locked in forward gear.

Unequal pay and job segregation are only part of the discrimination women experience in the workplace. Sexual harassment is another common abuse. According to an important November 1976 *Redbook* magazine survey, nine out of ten women reported experiencing sexual harassment on the job. Sylvia Lange, city editor of the *Winston-Salem Journal*, has provided this description of sexual harassment: "For some, it's a lewd remark...[or] being forced to listen to dirty jokes or obscene comments about other women in the office. For others, it's a pinch or a caress. It's a suggestion that a trip to bed will start the climb up the career ladder or threats that if sexual favors cease so will a job. And for still others, it's downright rape."[24]

Sexual harassment is a way to keep women in their place in the working world. It is a way to intimidate women workers from demanding their legal rights or organizing for better conditions, and it punishes women who quit their jobs out of fear and frustration and end up in lower-paying jobs or on welfare. As Lange explains, "The message women get is clear: you are more important as a sex object than you are as a worker."

Childcare

Childcare is one of the worst problems to confront women trying to hold a job outside the home. As of 1981, almost half of all women with children under 6 were in the paid labor force along with two-thirds of all women with kids between the ages of 6 and 17.[25] Some women work out childcare exchanges with friends and nearby relatives. Others rely on paid babysitters or use private or public daycare centers, *if* they can afford them and *if* they can find them.

There is a critical shortage of affordable, quality childcare services. According to the National Black Child Development Institute only 15 percent of all pre-school children were enrolled in licensed childcare services in 1980. Since then the Reagan Administration has reduced funding for non-profit childcare centers, as more and more working mothers depend upon them. The impact on the black community is especially serious since black children account for 44 percent of the total enrollment in federally-funded childcare programs.[26]

By 1990, calculates the National Black Child Development Institute, two-thirds of all mothers with children under six will be

LNS

employed outside the home and three million pre-schoolers will need childcare services. Current policy is undermining the (inadequate) services which do exist and insuring a crisis of escalating proportions for working mothers in years to come.

Childcare programs are being affected indirectly by cuts in other social services, as well as through direct cuts in childcare funding. Representative Paul Simon of Illinois told this story last year in his congressional newsletter:

> The Shawneetown Day Care Center operated in Gallatin County, a small Illinois county with high unemployment. The day care center struggled to get by and managed to do so, in part, because one CETA employee was assigned to it. When that CETA employee was cut off, the center couldn't continue. It folded.
>
> The result: The former CETA employee is now drawing unemployment compensation; the four women who were full-time employees of the day care center are drawing unemployment compensation; four of the women who were able to work because they had a place to leave their children have had to quit their jobs and go on welfare.
>
> And so the bottom line: One CETA employee's salary saved, and nine added to the welfare and unemployment compensation rolls...[27]

Jobs: The Case of the "Disappearing Middle"

> Part of the unemployment is not as much recession as it is the great increase in the people going into the job market, and ladies I'm not picking on anyone, but because of the increase in women who are working today and two-worker families and so forth.
>
> President Ronald Reagan,
> April 16, 1982 news conference

Childcare can make it possible for women with children to participate in the paid workforce and affirmative action can help women out of the "pink collar" ghetto. But occupational desegregation is no longer an effective, long-term response to women's poverty. In the coming years the U.S. job market will change dramatically as intermediate-level jobs are eliminated. The skilled trades, which offered generations of European immigrant men a way out of poverty, have been going the way of the watchmaker.

In a 1981 study of the labor market, professor Emma Rothschild of the Massachusetts Institute of Technology (MIT) found that 70 percent of all new private sector jobs created between 1973 and 1980 were low-paid, mostly "women's jobs" in the retail and service sectors (fast-food counter jobs, for example). Rothschild

Pat Murray/LNS

Table 3

Unemployment Rates 1970-1982

	1970	1975	1977	1979	1980	1981	1982
All Workers (16 & over)	4.9	8.5	7.1	5.8	7.1	7.6	9.7
White	4.5	7.8	6.2	5.1	6.3	6.7	8.6
Male	4.0	7.2	5.5	4.5	6.1	6.5	8.8
Female	5.4	8.6	7.3	5.9	6.5	6.9	8.3
Black	na	14.8	14.0	12.3	14.3	15.6	18.9
Male	na	14.8	13.3	11.4	14.5	15.7	20.1
Female	na	14.8	14.9	13.3	14.0	15.6	17.6
Latin (20 & over)	na	12.2	10.1	8.3	10.1	10.4	13.8
Male	na	11.4	9.0	7.0	9.7	10.2	13.6
Female	na	13.5	11.9	10.3	10.7	10.8	14.1
Women Maintaining Families	5.4	10.0	**9.4**	**8.3**	**9.2**	**10.4**	**11.7**
White	4.8	8.9	8.1	7.0	7.1	7.3	8.6
Black	7.5	14.0	16.4	12.9	14.9	16.8	18.7
Latin	na	15.9	14.0	12.4	14.6	12.0	16.7
Teenagers (16-19)	15.3	19.9	17.8	16.1	17.8	19.6	23.2
White	13.5	17.9	15.4	14.0	15.5	17.3	20.4
Black	na	39.5	41.1	36.5	38.5	41.4	48.0
Latin	na	27.7	22.9	19.2	22.5	24.0	29.9
Blue Collar Workers	6.2	11.7	8.1	7.0	10.0	10.3	14.2
White Collar Workers	2.8	4.7	4.3	3.4	3.7	4.0	4.9

Sources: U.S. Department of Labor, Bureau of Labor Statistics, "Labor Force Statistics Derived from the Current Population Survey: A Databook," Bulletin 2096, September 1982 and Employment and Earnings, January 1983; Census Bureau, Marital and Family Characteristics by Labor Statistics, unpublished.

Sophie Rivera

concludes that the United States "is moving toward a structure of employment ever more dominated by jobs that are badly paid, unchanging and unproductive."[28] The semi-skilled and skilled jobs that women might have advanced into are rapidly disappearing.

An important factor in this loss of skilled jobs is the shift in the U.S. economy known as "deindustrialization." U.S.-based factories are producing less cars, rubber, steel and other basic manufacturing goods. Many *relatively* well-paid blue collar jobs have been lost. Today one-third of all auto workers and one-half of all steel workers are out of work, with little prospect of renewed employment in the industries. The companies blame the workers for exhorbitant wages, but the real wages of U.S. workers have dropped so much in recent years that the average worker's paycheck now has less purchasing power than that of 1956.[29]

Many of the companies crying the loudest about uncompetitive wages have invested heavily overseas in search of lower taxes, sub-U.S. minimum wage costs and higher profits. Many of those "foreign" goods we see are made in factories owned wholly or in part by U.S.-based *Fortune* 500 companies. Not just auto and steel producers, but also manufacturers of garments, footwear, electronic appliances and other light-assembly products have moved in droves to Third World countries, such as Guatemala and the Philippines, where unions are prohibited or government-controlled, wages are kept at or below subsistence levels and health and safety regulations are weak or nonexistent. As the Institute for New Communications' pamphlet, *Women In the Global Factory*, points out, women comprise 80 to 90 percent of the Third World light-assembly workforce, earning $3 to $5 a *day* often under extremely repressive governments backed by the United States.

Overseas investment isn't the only reason for the decline in skilled manufacturing jobs in the United States. Automation and management's continual efforts to "streamline" the production process in order to maximize profit have also had great impact. In his 1974 study, *Labor and Monopoly Capital*, Harry Braverman explained that this streamlining of production took place at the expense of higher-paid, higher-skilled work.[30] Complicated tasks such as constructing a car were broken down into isolated steps performed repeatedly by workers stationed at posts along the assembly line. As management perfected this assembly line process, skilled mechanics and craftspeople who could perform all the steps lost their jobs. The assembly line workers who took their place were paid at a lower rate. Now, with rapid advances in automation and robot technology even the lowest paid line workers can be replaced.

Economist Bennett Harrison supports Braverman's findings with his own study of the New England economy. "The reorganization of work that occurs with the introduction of new automation equipment tends to eliminate jobs at the center of the skill spectrum. We call it a case of the disappearing middle. You have more low-skilled jobs at the bottom—jobs that are likely to be slotted for women—and then you have managerial jobs at the top, and a growing polarization between them."

The emerging picture is one of increased exploitation and despair. Anno Lee Saxenian, an editorial board member of the monthly economic magazine, *Dollars & Sense*, comments "We may be approaching a stituation like that in some Third World industrializing countries where there has been a big increase in jobs for women, but the jobs don't lead anywhere. They don't lift women out of poverty."

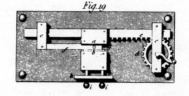

CHAPTER 3

THE "COMPASSIONATE STATE"?

Blaming the Victim

One of the most deep-rooted and damaging myths about poverty is that the poor are to blame for their plight. Poor single mothers are special targets in the blame-the-victim game.

In the mid-1960s, when female-headed households were widely viewed as an essentially black phenomenon, the well-publicized Moynihan Report, *The Negro Family: The Case for National Action*, put the blame for black poverty squarely on black women (Daniel Patrick Moynihan, now Senator from New York, became President Nixon's chief domestic policy advisor in 1969). Moynihan's "black matriarchy" theory argued that poverty in the black community was the result of black women dominating their families and, in effect, emasculating black men. Overwhelmed by "matriarchs" since the time of slavery, black men, said Moynihan, were unable to assume the male's rightful place as breadwinner at the head of the family.

Barbara Omolade, an historian with the Center for Worker Education at the City College of New York and a community organizer, points out how theories like Moynihan's add to the stigmatization of black single mothers: "Black women household heads struggle on the outside, for basic survival, and also on the inside, for self-worth."

The Sisterhood of Black Single Mothers was founded ten years ago in Brooklyn, New York to develop support systems for black single mothers and for the black community as a whole. The Sisterhood works with teenage mothers and their families, counsels women on issues related to education, jobs, health and housing, and acts as a referral group for other community organizations and agencies. Khadijah Matin, co-coordinator of the Sisterhood's Big Apple Project, explains, "We're trying to get people to take steps

Chip Berlet/LNS

toward self-determination and awareness, and to make positive links with existing institutions such as schools."

Self-determination for black women is the last thing today's self-styled, white male "experts" on black poverty want. In his book, *Wealth and Poverty*, New Right theoretician George Gilder asserts, "Any increase in the independence of black women, secured both by welfare and by jobs, will only further expand the appalling percentages of black children raised without fathers."[31] Following Moynihan, Gilder assumes that if black women would become more subservient to men within (and outside) the family, black poverty would wither away.

Robert H. Hill, author of the National Urban League study, "Economic Policies and Black Progress," provides a quick dose of reality: black families headed by women are poor "not because they do not have husbands, but because they do not have jobs."[32] Or, just as likely, the jobs they do have, don't pay enough. In 1981 black single mothers had an average yearly income of $6,907—well below the official poverty threshold.[33]

Hit with the double discrimination of racism and sexism, black women have remained on the bottom of an economic ladder with lower and lower rungs. In the last decade, the real income (after accounting for inflation) of the median black family declined by 5 percent to $12,674 as the gap between black and white income widened. In 1967 a black woman was 7.5 times as likely to be poor as a white man. In 1979 the ratio was changed for the worse: a black woman was 10 times as likely to be poor.[34]

From 1970 to 1980 the number of black households headed by women rose from 30 percent to 41 percent of all black families. During the same period the number of black families with no employed member doubled.[35] The black community as a whole is in a severe economic depression with overall unemployment over 20 percent and unemployment among youths recorded officially at 52 percent. Black women aren't the cause of poverty in the black community anymore than women in Flint, Michigan are the cause of lengthening unemployment lines there.

George Gilder and the Right extend their attack on female-headed households to all women. Their crusade for a better America involves a more general assault on the welfare state and women who have any economic and social independence. Women's work is in the home (unless, of course, their careers further rightwing causes). "The only dependable route from poverty," says Gilder, "is always work, family, and faith."[36] And for the Right, a family isn't a family if it's not headed by a man. Kathleen Teague, a leader in Phyllis Schlafly's STOP-ERA campaign and director of the New Right's American Legislative Exchange Council, wants to see women make more of an effort to attract husbands: "The only reason women aren't remarrying is that they don't have the right strategy... Some single women are trying to be martyrs, to prove they can be independent, that they can do anything. It would be better to say, 'How much I'd like to find a nice man!' Many men tell me how turned off they are by women who are trying so hard to be independent."

In the rightwing scheme of things, public assistance undermines the natural pact between the sexes and perpetuates poverty. In traditional marriage, explains Gilder, "the man disciplines his sexuality and extends it into the future through the womb of a woman. The woman gives him access to his children, otherwise forever denied him, and he gives her the product of his labor, otherwise dissipated on temporary pleasures."

When the state intervenes through welfare, the balance is upset, with the resulting loss of "male confidence and authority...The man has the gradually sinking feeling that his role as provider, the definitive male activity from the primal days of the hunt...has been largely seized from him; he has been cuckolded by the compassionate state."[37] And when a man doesn't feel needed by a wife, says Gilder, he is apt to be lazy, self-indulgent and violent. In short, Gilder's mandate for women is—in the words of Frank Ackerman, author of *Reaganomics: Rhetoric vs Reality*—"to stay home and play Beauty taming the Beast."[38]

Welfare Is No Game

The reality of welfare bears little in common with Gilder's "compassionate state" (we'll let men deal with Gilder's sordid view of the male gender) or the "lazy, welfare freeloader" stereotypes. Of all welfare recipients, 93 percent are women and children. Some four million women and eight million children now receive AFDC (Aid to Families with Dependent Children). And the reason there aren't more is that the system discourages all but the most desperate and determined from relying on welfare.

Marcy May, head organizer with RAM (Redistribute America Movement), a New York State welfare rights group with a membership of 6,000, mostly welfare mothers, describes the welfare welcome: "First you fill out a 14-page application and try and dig up old leases (assuming you had landlords who gave you leases), birth certificates and other documents. Then there's a 30-day processing period during which you get no support. When you come back after 30 days, they say, 'You're still alive—you don't need welfare.' "

Sally Michaels laughed as she recalled breezing into a Massachusetts welfare office: "Hi, I'm Sally Michaels. Do you have any brochures I could read?" Elizabeth C. (not her real name) stormed out of an Oregon welfare office after going through a typical runaround: "They had me wait with my infant son for hours, then sent me across town to another office to fill out more forms. I waited there for an hour or so, and then returned to the main desk, only to be given another form by the same clerk and directed back across town. I threw a fit. 'Why didn't you give me both forms at the same time?' I asked them.

"They accused me of not conducting myself properly and warned that I'd have to learn to behave like a welfare client if I wanted to get some assistance. I demanded my application and told them I never wanted to see them again. They're not human. They don't treat us as humans." At the time, Elizabeth's only alternative was traveling with her infant son to pick cherries, hoping that neither of them got sick or injured.

A 1978 study shows that AFDC use peaks a full two years after divorce or separation, demonstrating how hard women struggle to make it without going on welfare.[39] Once on the rolls, many become locked into a situation which Diana Pearce describes as a "workhouse without walls." Never having enough to get ahead, or even to meet daily expenses, many welfare recipients bounce back and forth between temporary low-paid work and public assistance, often using both simultaneously to sustain themselves and their families. In recent years, one-quarter of all AFDC recipients have been

working poor, employed in year-round, full-time jobs which don't provide enough income for subsistence. Only 12 percent of all recipients are "chronic," meaning they have been on welfare for four out of the past seven years.[40]

Humiliation is a permanent feature of welfare use. Carmen Gonzales, now a paid welfare advocate in Brooklyn, New York, first went on welfare for 18 months after her marriage broke up and she lost her job as a hair stylist. She has three children, but never saw any child support. Carmen managed to get off welfare with the help of WISH (the displaced homemaker's program mentioned earlier).

"Welfare was throwing me crumbs," Carmen explained. "It was so dehumanizing. I would cry whenever I came home and my kids would ask, 'Mama, what's wrong?' I just had to be alone for a while afterwards because it was so degrading. I felt like a hungry dog going to the welfare office to get a very little bone."

The little bone is getting even smaller with round after round of budget cuts. The "real value" of AFDC benefits (taking inflation into account) declined 29 percent between 1969 and 1981. The average AFDC payment was $93 per person, per month in 1979 (or $4,465 per year for a family of four). Payments are so low nationwide that in only three states do AFDC benefits *plus* foodstamps bring a household *up to* the poverty threshold. In Mississippi, the state with the lowest payments, the monthly allotment was $26 per person in 1979; in New York, one of the higher-paying states, the monthly allotment was $119 per person. In 1980, 26 states provided less than $300 in monthly AFDC payments to families of three (the average size family on welfare), and only 9 states provided more than $400 a month (or $4,800 per year).[41]

With pre-Reagan "hand-outs" like these, it's not hard to see why some welfare recipients work off the books. Carmen Gonzales told us that while on welfare she either had to bring in additional income from an unreported job or not have enough to feed her children.

Certain employers depend upon welfare recipients like Carmen Gonzales. William Tabb, professor of economics at Queens College, explains that "employers [in the garment industry, for example] lay off workers—mainly women—knowing that the workers will collect benefits to subsist and be available for rehiring. Thus, employers insure themselves a relatively stable but low-paid workforce." Workers are often rehired under the table at a fraction of their previous salaries.

Women working these kinds of jobs move in and out of the paid labor force with great frequency because of the financial insecurity of both welfare and their paid employment. If welfare payments covered basic needs, women would have some leverage to refuse underpaid and inconsistent employment. As it is, the jobs they hold include none of the benefits of more highly paid positions (which accrue seniority, health insurance, pensions) and often have terrible health and safety records. Many underemployed women must depend on welfare as a form of unemployment compensation (regular unemployment compensation requires a certain number of months at the same job) and as a way to get health insurance. In many states welfare is a requirement for Medicaid, and Medicaid is often the only form of health insurance the women can get for themselves and their children.

Workfare: "Modern Day Slave Market"

Workfare is a prime example of how the poor are punished for their poverty. The idea behind workfare is that welfare recipients

Family Income 1980

	All Races		White	
	All Families	Female Householder*	All Families	Female Househo
Median Income	$21,023	$10,408	$21,904	$11,908
Percent				
under $5,000	6.2	22.0	4.9	18.2
$5,000-9,999	12.7	26.3	11.3	23.5
$10,000-14,999	14.2	19.0	13.9	19.7
$15,000-24,999	27.7	21.8	28.3	24.9
$25,000-49,999	32.6	10.0	34.4	12.3
$50,000 & over	6.7	0.9	7.2	1.3

* Female head of household, with no husband present.

Source: *Statistical Abstracts*, citing U.S. Bureau of the Census, *Current Population Reports*, Seri "work off their debt to society" by putting in time at minimum wage jobs or in so-called job searches. The larger the welfare "debt," the more the recipients have to work to pay it off; so that the more needy you are, the more you are exploited. The Reagan Administration is encouraging states to impose workfare requirements and has proposed tying welfare to workfare as a matter of federal policy.

Sandra Helling, coordinator of the Public Work Project of the Welfare Grant Increase Coalition in New York sees the imposition of workfare as the "beginnings of a slave market of modern day slaves without rights."[42]

Workfare participants are employed in either the private or public sector at a wage rate less than or equal to the minimum wage. They have none of the rights or benefits of a regular job such as grievance procedures, Social Security credit, sick leave, workers compensation or the right to organize. Welfare recipients are exempted from workfare only if they are physically or mentally handicapped or if they have very young children—under two or three years of age, in some cases; under six in others. There are no provisions for childcare in the workfare scheme, with one exception: some programs have attempted to use workfare participants as unlicensed childcare workers for other participants' children. Many women, of course, are on welfare in the first place because they cannot find or afford childcare services to allow them to work outside the home.

Workfare is portrayed as a program to reinforce the "work ethic" and promote jobs, but there is no attempt to train and place

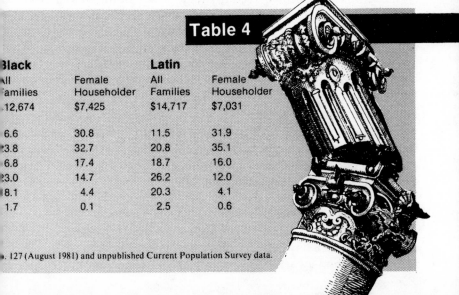

Table 4

| Black | | Latin | |
All Families	Female Householder	All Families	Female Householder
12,674	$7,425	$14,717	$7,031
6.6	30.8	11.5	31.9
3.8	32.7	20.8	35.1
6.8	17.4	18.7	16.0
23.0	14.7	26.2	12.0
8.1	4.4	20.3	4.1
1.7	0.1	2.5	0.6

127 (August 1981) and unpublished Current Population Survey data.

people on long-term career tracks. Indeed, many people have been forced back onto welfare with the elimination of CETA and other job programs. Frank Ackerman explains that the workfare "program ignores the question of whether the job represents a long-term solution to welfare dependence. In a pilot program in Lowell, Massachusetts, more than 50 recipients complained that they had been forced to interrupt other training programs, some at the college level, which would have given them a chance to find permanent, skilled jobs. Instead, because of the low pay and high turnover in their 'jobs club' [workfare] placements, they may find themselves back on welfare in a few months."[43]

On top of this, workfare is unfair to other workers. The National Welfare Rights Coalition, a national network of some 30 organizations, finds that workfare is used to displace paid public and private employees, shrink state and city payrolls, undermine prevailing wage rates and collective bargaining agreements and weaken labor unions.

The Workers' Rights Institute of Milwaukee, Wisconsin found that during a four-year pilot project 900 regular private and public employees were replaced by workfare participants who sometimes earned less than the minimum wage. The Institute concluded: "If in a small, industrialized, heavily unionized city like Milwaukee, 900 workers in industry can lose their jobs to a limited workfare program, the wholesale destruction of employment standards can be projected" under the Reagan Administration's plan of national, mandatory workfare.

Even as a device to recoup welfare expenditures and have recipients "pay off their debt to society," workfare doesn't work. All 20 states which have tried workfare have concluded that the programs are ineffective and cost more to administer than is gained in recipients' earnings.[44] However, as a device to reduce welfare *rolls*, workfare is very effective. Explains RAM founder Theresa Funicello: "In every state where workfare has been used, the rolls have been reduced, because for every welfare recipient put on workfare, approximately three others are cut off welfare altogether. In the long run workfare saves the government money by harassing and intimidating people who need welfare to such a point that either they drop out or they are disqualified."

Turning Back the Clock

The rights of poor and working people are threatened in two other areas which have direct impact upon women: "free enterprise zones" and "homework." The main feature of the "free enterprise zone" scheme is to reward companies with huge tax breaks for investing in targeted areas. Liberal supporters of the plan see it as a way of bringing business into poor inner-city areas where unemployment is high. Conservatives advocate additional measures—reduced minimum wage requirements, health and safety standards and environmental protections—as part of an overall effort to deregulate the economy and roll back the gains of workers and communities. While "free enterprise zones" legislation is bogged down at the federal level, meeting heavy resistance from labor, 14 states including Connecticut and Louisiana (the state recently cited as having the most toxic waste dumps) have already passed legislation to establish the zones with generous tax breaks.[45]

The creation of "free enterprise zones" could well result in sweatshop colonies. Economist William Goldsmith of Cornell University predicted in a recent study that the kinds of jobs produced in the zones will be low-paid, light-assembly work (garment, electronics, toys, etc.)—the kind of jobs seen as "women's work." Free enterprise zones, says Goldsmith, "could serve as vehicles through which an increasingly disenfranchised and desperate group of women could be massively exploited in the labor market."

Another vehicle for profitably exploiting women's labor is homework—and it's not the learning kind. Growing numbers of women would do industrial or clerical work without ever leaving

Tom Barry/LNS

their homes. There would be no way of regulating wages, work hours and health and safety conditions, and many workers would end up paying business overhead expenses such as equipment and materials.

The New Right justifies homework as a solution to the "breakdown of the family." "Business should be able to provide jobs that women can do without leaving their homes, like micro-electronics," insists Connie Marshner, chairperson (our term, not hers) of the Pro Family Coalition and editor of the *Family Protection Reporter*.

Homework was restricted under the Fair Labor Standards Act of 1938 after dedicated organizing against such long-standing abuses as 14-hour days/7-day weeks required to fill impossible piecework quotas. Labor unions don't want to see the clock turned back to the 19th century and are fighting efforts to loosen existing homework regulations. Illegal homework continues to thrive in the garment industry thanks to lax enforcement by the Department of Labor. The *New York Times* of March 3, 1981 told of Rosa, an undocumented worker from Ecuador who lives in a basement room in Union City, New Jersey, with her two children, one of whom is brain damaged. Rosa works 12 hours or more a day, 7 days a week, making shirts for 20 cents a piece. The contractors who buy the shirts often cheat her. Like millions of other undocumented workers from Latin America, the Caribbean and Asia, Rosa lives in constant fear of deportation, making her especially vulnerable to employment exploitation.

To make matters worse, homework may be the foot in the door to child labor—which is still a great problem in migrant farmwork. When questioned about the danger of a resurgence in child labor, Connie Marshner was unconcerned. "I'm not for child labor," she said, "but if the mother had a computer terminal at home and she had a 12 year old to help, I'd say, 'why not?' The humanistic reforms of the 19th century made children into economic liabilities."

CHAPTER 4

"REAGAN HOOD TAKES FROM THE NEEDY AND GIVES TO THE GREEDY"

That popular slogan sums up the consistent pattern of the Reagan Administration budget policy. Billions of dollars in budget cuts for social programs have gone hand in hand with massive tax breaks for big business and the wealthy and an unprecedented, unnecessary and dangerous military build-up. As a result of new tax provisions and cuts in benefit programs, households with incomes below $10,000 will lose $16.8 billion between 1983 and 1985 while those with incomes above $80,000 will gain $55.6 billion.

According to the Center on Budget and Policy Priorities, programs for which people must have low incomes to qualify or in which most beneficiaries are poor represent only ten percent of the federal budget (AFDC, food stamps, Medicaid, Legal Services, etc.). Yet these programs have been hit hardest by the budget cutbacks: "In fiscal year 1983, appropriations for these programs have been reduced to less than $82 billion. This represents a 28 percent reduction in two years, after adjusting for inflation." (The reduction would have been 45 percent if Reagan had gotten congressional approval for all the proposed 1983 cuts.)

Trickle Up Economics

What about the impact of the Economic Tax Recovery Act of 1981 and 1982 tax legislation? Households with incomes over

VIEW FROM THE TOP:
MULTIMILLIONAIRES AND THE
TRICKLE DOWN THEORY*

"A family with $10 million or so—not big wealth by today's standards—can readily live, and in fact many do live, as well as most of the country's centimillionaires...

"You don't need fabulous wealth to live very, very well these days. How many Rolls-Royces ($115,000 each) or yachts ($500,000 and up) do you really need or even *want*, after all? A year's worth of very fine dinners for two at gourmet restaurants costs about $50,000—the income from $400,000 in tax-exempt bonds, hardly great wealth. And your very own transatlantic jet seems superfluous when you can hop on the Concorde ($1,800, one way, New York to Paris).

"So what do the *really* rich do with their money? Some they give away: Philanthropy is 'in' among the very wealthy. But most of it is reinvested, either in their existing businesses, or stocks and bonds, or in new ventures. The main thing they do, then, is create jobs and ever more of the goods and services needed to sustain the average man's lifestyle, all in the search for profit, or sense of achievement by their own standards, or sense of family duty to the fortune. In a purely moral sense, then, conspicuous consumption may be 'obscene,' but great wealth is not."

The *Forbes* Four Hundred
September 13, 1982

* The richest people in the U.S. are *billionaires*: shipping magnate Daniel Keith Ludwig, oil tycoons like Gordon Peter Getty (son of John Paul Getty) and the Hunt family.

Millionaires represent a quarter of one percent of the U.S. population (according to a study by the U.S. Trust Corporation cited in the *New York Times*, June 28, 1979).

Steve Sack/The Minneapolis Tribune

$80,000 a year—about 5 percent of all households—will reap the lion's share of the "across-the-board" tax cuts, receiving tax reductions averaging $20,000 *a year* by 1985 *plus* additional savings from new tax shelter provisions.*[46] Most taxpayers will save little (under $30 in 1983) and many will wind up paying *more*, in part because of increased Social Security payroll taxes and increased consumption taxes. Since white-male-headed households have generally higher incomes, they will gain most from the tax windfall. Corporations, meanwhile, are paying a dwindling percentage of federal tax revenues: the corporate share dropped from 30 percent in 1940 to 12 percent in 1980 to 7.5 percent in 1982. President Reagan has suggested abolishing corporate taxes altogether.

As part of their 1981 "Welfare for the Rich" campaign, members of the Redistribute America Movement (RAM) protested a multimillion-dollar tax write-off for Tiffany's, the jewel of the jewelry business in New York City. They presented Tiffany's with a holiday gift, a baby doll frozen in an ice block wrapped in ribbon. "We wanted to give them something from the poor, so that they would know what their tax breaks mean—more poverty for us and our kids," explains RAM activist Sharon Hunt. A mother of five, Hunt has twice been forced to go on welfare because of underpaid jobs and inadequate childcare. She said that as a result of her participation in the welfare rights movement, "I no longer blame myself for being poor. I understand what's going on in this country." And it's not the trickle down in goods and services—from the "productive" rich to the "less productive" poor—that Reagan promises. As another welfare mother put it at the Tiffany's demonstration, "About the only thing that trickles down on us is the water from the apartment upstairs—when the building *has* running water."

Reagan didn't start the retreat from government responsibility for social welfare. Marcy May explains that "some of the most punishing initiatives carried out by the Reagan Administration, such as workfare and income-eligibility changes, were actually developed in Carter's 1977 welfare 'reform' proposal." But Reagan has led the retreat at a gallop, attacking the principles of the welfare state as well as the cost. Only for the "truly needy"—a tiny group of "deserving poor," defined and redefined at the whim of the Reagan Administration—would there be a "social safety net."

For fiscal year 1984, Reagan proposed a federal spending "freeze." This, like "across-the-board tax cut," is another term for trickle up. Social welfare programs are to be slashed again. In his January 1983 State of the Union address, Reagan repeated his claim that food stamps and other social welfare "uncontrollables" were the cause of the federal deficit—even as he proposed a 14 percent hike in military spending.

Food and Nutrition Programs on the Chopping Block

President Reagan likes to shock people with the fact that food

"Hey, WIMP! . . . Whatcha got in the lunch pail?"

Doug Marlette/The Charlotte Observer

stamps have increased 16,000 percent over the last 15 years—neglecting to mention that back in 1966 the food stamp program was a tiny pilot project, launched in response to evidence of widespread hunger and malnutrition. Today, one out of ten Americans participate in the food stamp program, making it one of the most important supports for the working and nonworking poor.

About 80 percent of those on food stamps are single mothers, children, the elderly or disabled. Food stamp households have

Changes in Household Income
as a Result of Budget Cuts and Tax Provisions
Fiscal Years 1981 and 1982

	Households with incomes under $10,000*	Households with incomes over $80,000
1983	- 5.8 billion	. $14.4 billion
1984	- $6.1 billion	+ $19.0 billion
1985	- $4.9 billion	+ $22.2 billion

Table 6

* These figures actually understate the losses to low income households because they reflect budget cuts only in benefit programs and not in services programs such as social services, health services and legal services. For example, these figures do not reflect increased day care fees that many low income working households must now pay as a result of cuts in programs providing support for day care centers in poor areas.

Source: Robert Greenstein, with John Bickerman, of the Center on Budget and Policy Priorities, *The Effect of the Administration's Budget, Tax, and Military Policies on Low Income Americans*, (Washington D.C.: Interreligious Task Force on U.S. Food Policy, February 1983), citing Congressional Budget Office, *Effects of Tax and Benefit Reductions Enacted in 1981 for Households in Different Income Categories*, February 1982 and *Effects of Changes in Taxes and Benefit Payments Enacted in Fiscal Year 1982, for Households in Different Income Categories*, November 1982.

Su Friedrich/LNS

average gross incomes of $349 a month.[48] With unemployment and poverty on the rise, the food stamp rolls should be growing. But they aren't. Since Reagan took office, some one million recipients have been terminated, nearly all others are receiving reduced benefits and new eligibility restrictions have kept many potential food stamp users out of the program.

Samuel J. Cornelius, administrator of the Federal Food and Nutrition Service, considers most current recipients to be undeserving and not "truly needy." In an interview last year Cornelius asserted, "We have 22.3 million people on food stamps. Of that 22.3 million, four million are considered to be truly needy."[49] The other 18 million could be terminated.

Cornelius has defended cuts in the school lunch program with the assurance they would make "near-poor children bear a fair share of inflation." Earlier, the Food and Nutrition Service tried to reduce costs by reclassifying ketchup as a vegetable. As a result of cuts in the school lunch program three million fewer children are participating. The childcare food program, which subsidizes meals for mostly low-income daycare institutions, has been cut by 30 percent. Many of these same children are also feeling the impact of food stamp cuts. For fiscal 1984, the Reagan Administration proposed to merge the childcare, school breakfast and summer food programs into a block grant with a 28 percent cut in funding.

On the other end of the age scale, the Food and mal-Nutrition

Service has proposed changing the definition of elderly person from one who is 60 years and older to one who is 65 or more, saving money by terminating current recipients. Asked by a reporter whether the proposal might appear anti-elderly, Cornelius responded, "I'm sure it would be... The question is what we can pay for. There are some people between the ages of 60 and 65 who are millionaires."[50] Many people, namely one-fifth of all women over 60, are poor and many more are near-poor. Perhaps Cornelius was thinking of the Reagan Cabinet where being a millionaire is par for the course. But millionaires don't get food stamps; they get tax deductions for "business" meals and entertainment.

Critics are fond of anecdotes about people using food stamps to buy everything from caviar to Cadillacs. Linda Johnson of the New York-based Food and Hunger Hotline responds: "You can't buy toilet paper, toothpaste or Pampers with *food* stamps—so how are you going to buy a bottle of vodka, much less a Cadillac?" The average food stamp allotment per meal, per person is 47 cents—less than the price of a cup of coffee at a diner. No wonder, then, that a study by the U.S. Department of Agriculture found that food stamp recipients were far more economical and careful shoppers than non-food stamp shoppers. But, however much you save with coupons and steer away from junk food, 47 cents per meal doesn't go very far. It goes even less far in poor neighborhoods. A recent study of the Bronx by the Community Food Resource Center in New York found that in low-income areas food prices were significantly higher than in wealthier neighborhoods: 21 percent higher for milk and chicken; 31 percent for margarine. And, needless to say, the food stamp allotment doesn't include a travel allowance for comparison shopping.

The budget cuts and more restrictive eligibility requirements are taking a heavy toll. The Food and Hunger Hotline has seen a

sharp rise in calls for emergency food, starting right after the fiscal year 1982 budget went into effect in October 1981. Most of the Hotline's callers are women with children. Donna Lawrence, the Hotline's director, explains that "most are desperate. They've been to friends, families and the welfare center and we are their last resort. Many callers say they didn't eat the day before and their kids only get regular meals at school." Linda Johnson adds, "Some women are so desperate they have their kids placed in foster care so at least the kids are being fed until they get a job, or get their welfare and food stamps straightened out. And then the mothers have to fight to get their kids back."

Yet Samuel Cornelius wants greater proof of suffering. He told *Community Nutrition Institute Weekly* (June 24, 1982): "I've had experiences where people accuse me of...starving out the little children. But I have yet to see somebody say, 'Hey, Mr. Cornelius, you see the kid over there that's dead? The reason why he's dead is because you've starved him.' "

Children *are* dying because of the cutbacks. On January 23, 1983, CBS News did a report on the upsurge in low-weight births and infant mortality around the country, citing a study by the Washington-based Food Research and Action Center. The causes are cumulative: rising poverty and unemployment coupled with increasingly inadequate nutrition and preventative health programs. The Women-Infants-Children Food Program (WIC) is a good example of the gap between need and services. According to Dr. Bailus Walker, director of Public Health for Michigan, the state's WIC program has enough money to serve 76,000 families, but another 30,000 need it. Michigan, a state devastated by auto layoffs, is seeing, says Dr. Walker, "one of the greatest year-to-year increases" in infant mortality "since World War II."[51] The infant mortality rate of inner-city Detroit is higher than that of Honduras.

"If You Think the System is Working, Ask Someone Who Isn't"

By the winter of 1982, an estimated two million Americans were homeless—living in cars, subway stations and streetside cardboard boxes, or roaming the country in search of jobs in the "low unemployment" cities of the southwest. Many of the homeless are two-parent families or single mothers whose kids are missing school and subsisting off sugared cereal and punch mixes.

Some of the homeless are unemployed workers whose benefits have run out, or poor people dropped from the welfare rolls. Others are elderly women and men who have no pensions or Social Security, or their payments are too meager to cover food, medicine

"I've called the family together to announce that, because of inflation, I'm going to have to let two of you go."

and rent. Some are former mental patients who were released from institutions despite the lack of intended follow-up services, most of which were never established due to budget cutbacks. Still others were displaced from their low-rent apartments in the cycle of arson-for-profit, tax-supported co-op conversion and neighborhood gentrification known by its victims as "urban removal."

One of the only ways the homeless have to raise a little cash for food and other necessities is by selling blood to hospitals. But it's a buyers market. In Denver the price per donation has dropped from eight dollars to seven dollars. As one donor told the *New York Times* (December 25, 1982), "there's so many poor people, and they're all selling it."

Unemployment reached nearly 11 percent in 1983, which means that some 12 million Americans are officially counted as wanting a job, but not being able to find one. It is important to know that official unemployment statistics drastically understate conditions by excluding millions of would-be workers who have given up looking for work after months or years of fruitless search (discouraged workers) and by not counting part-time workers who need and want a full-time job, but cannot find one. Many discouraged and involuntarily part-time workers are women.

The average period of unemployment has lengthened considerably, but the duration of unemployment benefits has been shortened as a budget-cutting measure. According to the Center on Budget

Table 7

Budget Cutbacks in Low-Income Programs
Fiscal Years 1981-1984

After adjusting for inflation, proposed funding for the following programs represents a 40 percent reduction from FY 1981 levels and 19 percent below FY 1983 levels.

	FY 1981 Appropriations	FY 1983 Appropriations ($ in billions)	FY 1984 Proposed
AFDC	8.5	7.8	7.1
Food Stamps	11.3	12.8	11.7
Medicaid	17.4	19.3	20.8
SSI (Supplemental Security Insurance)	7.2	8.1	8.6
Subsidized Housing	24.8	8.7	-2.3
Employment & Training	7.9	4.1	3.6
Legal Services	0.3	0.2	0.0
Community Services	0.5	0.4	0.0
WIC	0.9	1.1	1.1
Free & Reduced-Price Meals	2.9	3.0	2.8
Maternal & Child Health	0.5	0.4	0.4
Primary Care & Migrant Health	0.4	0.3	0.3
Low-Income Energy Assistance	1.85	2.0	1.3
Compensatory Education	3.5	3.2	3.0
Financial Aid for Needy Students	3.8	3.6	3.6
Headstart	0.8	0.9	1.05
Child Welfare Services	0.5	0.6	0.6
Social Services	3.0	2.45	2.5
Veterans Pensions	3.8	3.8	3.8
Earned Income Tax Credit	1.3	1.2	1.1
TOTAL	101.15	83.95	71.05

Source: Center on Budget and Policy Priorities, Washington, D.C.

AFDC: Households headed by women account for 83 percent of all AFDC recipients. As a result of 1981 and 1982 cutbacks, 365,000 families have been terminated; an additional 260,000 families have had their benefits reduced. In nearly half of the states, AFDC recipients lose Medicaid coverage for themselves and their families when they are dropped from AFDC.

Food Stamps: Nearly 70 percent of all food stamp households are headed by women; over half of all beneficiaries are children. Cutbacks in 1981 and 1982 eliminated nearly one million food stamp recipients; most other recipients have had their allotments reduced. The U.S. Department of Agriculture has estimated that for every 1 percent rise in unemployment, the food stamp rolls should increase by one million persons. Because of cutbacks and more stringent eligibility requirements, however, the food stamp rolls have remained fairly stable in the face of rising unemployment. The Food Stamp program for Puerto Rico was replaced with a lump sum grant, amounting to a 25 percent reduction in funding.

Medicaid: Over 60 percent of those using Medicaid are women; about 40 percent of Medicaid funding goes to long-term care of the elderly, most of whom are women. An estimated 660,000 children lost Medicaid coverage when their families were terminated from AFDC. Many poor families must pay more out of their own pockets for medical services covered by Medicaid and coverage has been reduced in a variety of ways (e.g. in many states, Medicaid coverage of eyeglasses for poor children has been eliminated).

Subsidized Housing: About 66 percent of households using subsidized housing are headed by women. Most of the elderly in subsidized housing are women living alone. Rents have been increased from a maximum of 25 percent of annual income to 30 percent.

Public Service Employment: Public service jobs funded under the Comprehensive Employment and Training Act (CETA) have been eliminated. Over 60 percent of the 300,000 former CETA employees were women.

Legal Services: Women represent 67 percent of all Legal Services clients; 36 percent of the program's attorneys are women. Nearly one million clients have lost eligibility for Legal Services and another one million receive reduced services. The Reagan Administration has attempted to abolish the entire program. Recent restrictions prohibit Legal Services representation in class action suits and limit the representation of undocumented immigrants.

WIC (Women-Infants-Children Food Program): WIC currently serves two million women and children (under 5), reaching only an estimated one-third of all those identified as "nutritional risks." According to the *New York Times* of February 20, 1983, "Getting a WIC recipient through her pregnancy costs $450; getting a sick baby through a stint in a neonatal unit can cost the Government $40,000."

School Lunch Programs: Almost half of all children eligible for free or reduced-price lunches are in families headed by women. Three million children no longer participate in the school lunch program; 2,700 schools have dropped out.

Sources: Center on Budget and Policy Priorities (Washington, D.C.); Food Research and Action Center (Washington, D.C.); Food and Hunger Hotline (New York), Community Food Resource Center (New York); National Education Association, *Inequality of Sacrifice* (Washington, D.C.).

and Policy Priorities, "More than half of the 12 million unemployed now do not receive any unemployment benefits whatsoever...the situation is grim. Many of these persons cannot qualify for public assistance. More than half the states do not make welfare payments to families in which both parents are present....If these families are poor enough, they may be able to receive food stamps—but food stamp benefits average only about $10 per person per week."[52]

Still, it's called a recession and not a depression. Often the headlines and photo captions tell a truer story than the statistics: "10,000 Line Up in Baltimore Seeking 70 Federal Jobs" (*New York Times,* September 16, 1980). Mainstream economists such as Martin Feldstein, head of Reagan's Council on Economic Advisers, routinely speak of a permanent *structural* unemployment rate of six to seven percent, below which the economy will not run "efficiently." A rate of six to seven percent unemployment is half as much as today's figure, but *twice* as much as the old norm of "full employment" (at three to four percent unemployed). Amidst the deepest economic crisis since the Great Depression, millions of Americans are being doomed to *permanent* joblessness by the economically privileged.

Throwing Money at the Military

The money being stripped from human services is going to the military. The Reagan Administration has planned a five-year military buildup of $1.7 trillion. Already, over 50 cents of every dollar in federal income taxes goes to military-related spending.[53] The Reagan Administration says this megamilitary is necessary for "national security," but more is spent on military *bands* than is spent on the Endowments for the Arts and Humanities. And $3 million was spent in 1982 on veterinary care (Veticaid?) for the pets of the Pentagon generals.[54]

The American people have become more and more skeptical of the need for such a huge military machine and more and more worried about plans for a "prolonged nuclear war." So the Reagan Administration is also stressing the supposed economic benefits of militarism. Military spending, we are told, "creates jobs." But Marion Anderson of Employment Research Associates has indicated that the same billion dollars spent on the military would generate more jobs in the civilian sector—jobs which are more likely to go to women than those in high-tech military production. One billion dollars spent on guided missiles, for example, produces 14,000 jobs. One billion spent on hospitals and education produces, respectively, 48,000 and 62,000 jobs. In a 1980 study, Anderson found that women lost jobs in 49 out of 50 states as billions were spent on the military instead of in the civilian economy or for human services.[55]

Welfare rights and civil rights activists have long spoken of the "poverty draft" which drives poor people into the "All-Volunteer Army" in disproportionate numbers. With cutbacks in social spending and shrinking educational and job opportunities in the civilian economy, the poverty draft is intensifying. And to tighten the vise even further, the Reagan Administration has stopped paying unemployment benefits to military personnel who "quit their jobs voluntarily" by choosing not to reenlist. Brenda C. knows what the poverty draft means. As she explained at the beginning of this pamphlet, she joined the army in desperation, believing "It's my last chance to try and support my family."

Welfare for the Wealthy, Free Enterprise for the Poor

The Reagan Administration's rollback of vital social services is being carried out under the guise of getting "big government" off the backs of average taxpayers. "The attack on 'big government' is a rhetorical attack," explains Frances Fox Piven, a longtime activist in the welfare rights movement and coauthor of *The New Class War: Reagan's Attack on the Welfare State and Its Consequences.* "The only thing they're really attacking is the social welfare function of government," says Piven. "Neither the Republican Right nor the neoliberals are proposing to reduce the government activities that business depends on."[56]

A decade ago, George Wiley, the founding director of the National Welfare Rights Organization, wrote: "almost everyone in America is on welfare, except that it's called...'defense contracts' or 'guaranteed loans' or 'oil depletion allowances' or 'tax-free capital gains'—in short, socialism for the rich and free enterprise for the poor." Wiley concluded, "The choice we face as a nation is more than just welfare reform. We must choose what kind of people we want to be."[57]

CHAPTER 5

LOOKING BACK & LOOKING FORWARD

The short-lived "war on poverty" has become a war on the poor in which women and children are the main casualties. Yet cutbacks are not the *cause* of women's poverty—and neither is high unemployment. The feminization of poverty preceded the current depression and will persist even in the unlikely event of a sustained economic recovery. Women are the first fired, last hired and lowest paid in the best of times.

The feminization of poverty is a direct outgrowth of women's dual role as unpaid labor in the home and underpaid labor in the workforce. The pace has been quickened by rising rates of divorce and single motherhood, but the course of women's poverty is determined by the sexism—and racism—ingrained in an unjust economy.

Single mothers are in a constant state of economic crisis whether they are trying to support their children on jobs paying "pin money" wages or on public assistance, or a mixture of both. The crisis is compounded by inadequate childcare. The problem is not that there are growing numbers of female-headed households. The problem is the system which dooms one out of three of these households to poverty—and many more to near-poverty.

The New Right would like to stamp out women-headed households in a modern crusade to reassert the sovereignty of the male-dominated family. The so-called "Family Protection Act" would mandate Big Brother government to prohibit federal funding for battered women's programs and child abuse services; prohibit

Legal Services representation in cases involving divorce, abortion, school desegregation and lesbian and gay rights; provide tax exemptions for private, parent-run schools while excluding them from compliance with non-discrimination statutes; and defund schools which use educational materials that do not reinforce "traditional" sex role differences. The New Right solution is not only reactionary and authoritarian; it is also economically ludicrous. About half of all women with employed husbands are in the workforce in large part out of economic necessity. According to the Institute for Labor Education and Research, "The standard of living provided by the average worker's earnings was lower in 1981 than it was in 1956."[58]

Downward Mobility

For women, economic "recovery" does not spell relief. The "new" job opportunities for women are mainly variations on the old. The large corporations which dominate the economy are eliminating better-paying, middle-level jobs through automation and the reorganization of work and lowering wages and benefits with recession-induced "give backs." Meanwhile the ranks of underpaid workers in fast-food chains, word-processor pools and microcomputer assembly lines are swelling.

The labor market is becoming polarized between a privileged sector of managers and professionals, at the top, and an increasingly impoverished sector of wage workers with women at the bottom. At one end of the economic spectrum is the woman of color who earns less than $7,500 a year for full-time work. At the other end is the white male corporate executive who earns a yearly salary figured in the *millions:* In 1980, the 20 best-paid corporate executives earned between $1.5 million and $3.3 million a year in salary, bonus and long-term income (and that's not including unearned income from investments, inheritance, etc.).*

It's no coincidence that the political assault on social welfare is coming at a time of severe unemployment, for the more intense the competition for jobs and the more precarious the welfare system, the more precious is a job—any job. Economist William Tabb explains that administrations from Nixon's on have sought "to create space to transform the U.S. economy" in the interest of big

*According to the Institute for Labor Education and Research, "Between 1972—when it reached its postwar peak—and 1981, the purchasing power of the average worker's earnings declined by 16 percent." But the earnings of top corporate executives jumped by 18 percent (controlling for inflation) between 1976 and 1979.[59]

Ros Everdell/Solidarity Day Rally

business. "Space for change is created by...zapping labor—forcing down the real wages of U.S. workers and cutting the services they have come to expect from their government. Lowered expectations, the politics of less, benign neglect; these are the continuing policies which it is hoped will allow for a restructuring of economic relations."[60]

The promise of Reaganomics is that by giving more wealth to the wealthy, more prosperity will trickle down in a burst of renewed investment and production. Not surprisingly, Reaganomics has turned out to be as effective as giving more food to the overfed and promising the hungry more crumbs will fall off the table. In fact, new investment *declined* in 1982, factories have been running at less than 70 percent of capacity, corporations have been using tax windfalls and borrowed billions to buy up other companies in record-breaking mergers, and the rich have been on a luxury spending binge and speculation spree in real estate, paintings and other commodities. Communities and countries have been forced into a bidding war by multinational corporations playing harder and harder to get. Economist Barry Bluestone provides this example from General Motors' Poletown plant in Detroit:

> General Motors announces that they're going to close the two remaining Cadillac factories in Detroit. They're willing to build a new plant right in the city rather than shift a plant to Montgomery, Alabama, but they need some help: twelve-year, 50 percent tax abatement, 430 acres of land in the middle of the city, the

displacement of 3,200 residences, 160 businesses, nursing homes, and hospitals. They want the city to use eminent domain to clear what is a nonblighted neighborhood, and to pay for that...[61]

Toward a Feminist Economic Program

In an economic system which has been largely hostile, women have fought hard for government social welfare programs. It took decades to win widespread recognition of the right to subsistence and establish the welfare state as we know it, from AFDC to Social Security. These human services are flawed in many respects, distorted by a depersonalized bureaucracy and manipulated by business interests. But welfare programs have provided an essential means of economic survival for millions of women and children.

There's more at stake than government programs. In the 1970s, the women's movement identified problems that were previously seen as personal—rape, incest, battering and sexual harassment— and demanded solutions. Women built an impressive array of non-profit services such as health clinics and shelters for battered women. Often they provided innovative models of non-hierarchical, community-centered human services. But many of these grassroots institutions received federal support, in the form of CETA and VISTA workers, for example. Now, this entire network of alternative community-based programs is in jeopardy.

Where do we go from here? In order to alleviate the growing burden of women's poverty, we must fight to restore and expand government social welfare programs and preserve and strengthen grassroots institutions. But that is not enough. If we are to pull women out of the economic quicksand, once and for all, we must confront the inequality, sexism and racism which are so deeply entrenched in our economy and culture.

Sexism and racism limit women socially, economically and politically. Sexist attitudes, like the idea that women are working for "pin money" while men are working for a living, reinforce women's exploitation as cheap labor. Violence against women and sexual harassment are expressions of deeply ingrained attitudes and practices which can confront women anywhere—at home, on the street, at work. Racism has been a part of this country since Native Americans were first thrown off their lands and blacks were dragged here as slaves. It was not until 1954 that "separate but equal" was struck down as a legal principle and inequality remains pervasive today for blacks and other peoples of color. Racism and sexism help perpetuate the unjust system by dividing people who have common economic interests.

Tom Tuthill/LNS

Poverty and unemployment need not be permanent facts of economic life. But they will be, as long as we have a government which calls itself a democracy yet does not practice equality of rights, opportunity and treatment. The former chairman of President Johnson's Council of Economic Advisors has spoken bluntly about "the double standard of a capitalist democracy, professing and pursuing an egalitarian political and social system and simultaneously generating gaping disparities in economic well-being."

Capitalist institutions, he said, "award prizes that allow the big winners to feed their pets better than the losers can feed their children."[62] What follows are basic elements of a feminist economic program for *immediate* action:

●*Guaranteed Adequate Income:* We need a system of income support that assures every person a decent living *above* the poverty level. Welfare in the United States is deficient and degrading. But government income support programs do not have to be this way. Compare welfare to Social Security, which is financially inadequate, but not deliberately stigmatized. Income support programs should be administered in a dignified and client-centered manner.

●*Full Employment:* The current economic system is unable to provide jobs for all those who need, want and are able to work. There is a vast amount of work that urgently needs to be done and that could generate jobs for millions of people: providing accessible, quality healthcare, education, housing, childcare, recreation and other human services; constructing an effective mass transit system; cleaning up and protecting the environment; developing safe, renewable energy sources; etc. All people have the right to meaningful, socially constructive work that is safe and well-paid.

●*End To Employment Discrimination*: We need equal pay for comparable work; systematic affirmative action (not just affirmative tokenism); strict enforcement of legislation prohibiting discrimination on the basis of sex, race, age and sexual preference; and effective job training and retraining programs. Income support programs must insure that during job training participants and their families have an adequate living.

●*Childcare:* Childcare was one of the initial demands of the women's movement and we must reassert its critical importance. Childcare services are absolutely essential to working mothers. All

children have the right to healthy, educational, stable and supportive childcare services.

• *Reproductive Rights:* The assault on women's reproductive freedom is not "pro-life" as the rightwing claims, but anti-woman and anti-child. The government has cut off federal funding for abortion and severely restricted access to birth control services. Yet, at the same time, public and private hospitals continue to sterilize poor women with federal money, often without the women's consent. Not to mention that a truly pro-life program would fund pre-natal and child health and nutrition care for the millions of women and children who need it. The ability to plan wanted births and prevent unwanted births is fundamental to a women's health and dignity as well as her economic survival and that of any children she may already have.

• *Human Needs And Services:* No country can call itself a democracy when access to education, jobs, healthcare, housing, etc. are so skewed by race, sex and class background. Education through college should be free and equitable. Medicaid and Medicare are not enough. We need a national public health system in which *preventative* medicine is a priority—from personal nutrition to workplace and environmental health and safety.

A feminist economic program will require a major reordering of priorities and a democratic reconstruction of the economy. Under the present system, the costs of the economy are shared (toxic waste, inflation, unemployment, etc.) while the profits are heavily concentrated in a few hands: less than 2 percent of the population owns more than 30 percent of all privately-held wealth and more than half of all corporate stock. The country is hostage to the investment decisions of multinational corporations which monopolize our natural resources, food system and other essential life-support resources. Family farms are being driven out of business in

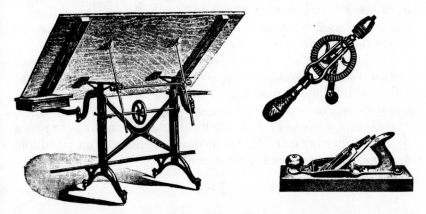

increasing numbers while more and more people are going hungry. Investment and production decisions that effect the lives of millions of people should be made democratically, not by a handful of corporate leaders. Democracy must be extended to the economy—from the shop floor up.

We need tax and budget policies that are designed to redistribute wealth *downwards* to the majority of the American people. We must reverse the shift in resources now taking place from human services to the military (one cruise missile costs $3.6 million, the equivalent of 3,600 Basic Educational Opportunity Grants at $1,000 a piece).[63] We can safely reduce military spending to a level necessary solely for *defense* by stopping production of offensive, first-strike nuclear weapons, pursuing nuclear and conventional disarmament and cutting off support to repressive regimes such as those in El Salvador, Guatemala and South Africa. The defense program we need most desperately as women is one which will protect us against the *domestic* dangers of poverty, sexism and racism.

The Reagan Administration targeted those groups expected to offer the least resistance—women and the poor. But a sign of women's dissatisfaction with present military and economic policies is the growing "gender gap" in voting patterns. Never before have women been recognized as so powerful a political force within the electoral arena. We need to use that power in the interests of all women: the poor and the not-yet poor. But certainly women cannot rely on electoral politics alone. Grassroots education and mobilization are essential. In Massachusetts, for example, Women for Economic Justice established a statewide women's welfare coalition which includes women from District 65 of the United Auto Workers, the Coalition of Battered Women's Service Groups, the Coalition for Basic Human Needs and others. Women for Economic Justice, says its director Jean Entine, is "attempting to build an organization of working class, low-income and middle class women" which unites, rather than divides women on the basis of economic issues.

Women have a long history of fighting for economic and social justice. Today the stakes are higher than ever. The challenge of the 1980s is to build multi-racial coalitions which bring together women's organizations with welfare rights, civil rights, labor, antiwar and other groups. Women can and will continue to play a decisive role in constructing a society centered not on greed and war, but on human needs and aspirations.

FOOTNOTES

1. See U.S. Department of Commerce, Bureau of the Census, "A Statistical Portrait of Women in the U.S.," *Current Population Reports*, Special Study, Series P. 23, No. 56, 1976, and Bureau of the Census, "Characteristics of the Population Below the Poverty Level," *Current Population Reports*, 1978, cited by Harriette McAdoo and Diana Pearce in "Women and Children: Alone and in Poverty" for the National Advisory Council on Economic Opportunity, Final Report, September 1981; *Current Population Survey* cited by the Children's Defense Fund, *A Children's Defense Budget: An Analysis of the President's Budget and Children*.
2. *New York Times*, December 19, 1982; Alexander Cockburn and James Ridgeway, *Village Voice*, March 1, 1983, p. 10-11.
3. Diana Pearce, "The Feminization of Poverty: Women, Work and Welfare," *Urban and Social Change Review*, February 1978; Statistics from an interview with Pearce, March 1982.
4. See Bureau of the Census, "Profile of the United States: 1981," *Current Population Reports*, Series P. 20, No. 374; Bureau of the Census, "Families Maintained by Female Headed Householders 1970-79," *Current Population Reports*, Series P. 23, No. 107, 1980.
5. Patricia C. Sexton, *Women and Work*, R. and D. Monograph, No. 46 (Washington, D.C.: U.S. Department of Labor, Employment and Training Administration, 1977), cited in The National Advisory Council on Economic Opportunity, *Final Report*.
6. Lenore J. Weitzman, "The Economics of Divorce: Social and Economic Consequences of Property, Alimony and Child Support Awards," UCLA *Law Review* No. 28 (November 1981), cited in Ellen Max, "Divorce is a Financial Disaster for Women and Children," *The Women's Advocate*, National Center on Women and Family Law, September 1982.
7. See Bureau of Labor Statistics, *Child Support Payments in the U.S.*, cited in WOW fact sheet on women; Barbara S. Cain, "The Gray Divorcee," *The New York Times Magazine*, December 19, 1982, pp. 89-97.
8. Urban Institute, Washington, D.C., "Child Support Payments in the U.S.," 1976 cited by Diana Pearce in "The Feminization of Poverty, *Urban and Social Change Review*.
9. Laws of New York, Chapter 717, effective August 5, 1977.
10. Lisa Henricksson, "Getting Better About Getting Older," *Family Circle*, January 1983, p. 2.
11. Cain, "The Plight of the Gray Divorcee," p. 92.
12. *Ibid.*
13. Bureau of the Census, *Current Population Reports*, Series P. 60, No. 125 (1979); Alexander Cockburn and James Ridgeway, *Village Voice*, March 1, 1983, pp. 10-11.
14. *New York Times*, November 15, 1982.
15. U.S. Department of Labor, Bureau of Labor Statistics, and Bureau of the Census, Annual Series P. 60, No. 125.
16. See fact sheet on women's poverty prepared by Wider Opportunities for Women (WOW), Women's Workforce Network, Washington, D.C.; Bureau of the Census, Annual Series P. 60, No. 125.
17. *New York Times*, November 15, 1982.
18. Diana Pearce, "The Feminization of Poverty," *Urban and Social Change Review*, February 1978.
19. Bureau of Labor Statistics, *Women in the Workforce*, No. 575.
20. See Bureau of Labor Statistics, *1981 Weekly Earnings of Men and Women Compared in 100 Occupations;* Census Bureau and Bureau of Labor Statistics, Annual Series P. 60, No. 125
21. Bureau of Labor Statistics, Series No. 647.
22. Debby Warren, "The Bottom Line: Union Women Get Paid From 19 Percent to 34 Percent More Than Their Sisters Who Are Not in Unions," *Southern Exposure*, Winter 1981, p. 84.
23. U.S. Department of Labor Women's Bureau, *The Earnings Gap Between Men and Women* (Washington, D.C.: 1979).

24. Sylvia Ingle Lane, "Speak Up, Speak Out, Say No," *Southern Exposure*, Winter 1981, p. 114.
25. *Newsweek*, January 17, 1983, pp. 20-32.
26. National Black Child Development Institute, *The Status of Black Children in 1990*, Washington, D.C., 1979; Ruopp, R. et al, *Children at the Center* (Cambridge, MA: Abt Associates, 1979).
27. *New York Times*, January 22, 1982.
28. Emma Rothschild, "Reagan and the Real America," *New York Review of Books*, February 5, 1981.
29. Institute for Labor Education and Research, *We Are Not the Problem!* New York, 1982.
30. Harry Braverman, *Labor and Monopoly Capital: The Degradation of Work in the Twentieth Century* (New York: Monthly Review Press, 1974).
31. George Gilder, *Wealth and Poverty* (New York: Basic Books, 1981), p. 135.
32. Robert H. Hill, *Economic Policies and Black Progress: Myths and Realities* (Washington D.C.: National Urban League, Research Department, 1981), p. 22.
33. Paul Glick, "A Demographic Picture of Black Families," from Harriette McAdoo, ed. *Black Families* (Beverly Hills: Sage Press, 1981).
34. See Census Bureau, *Current Population Reports*, Money Income and Poverty Status of Families and Persons in the United States, Series P-60, No. 125 (1979); *New York Times*, April 25, 1982.
35. See Census Bureau, *Current Population Reports*, Families Maintained by Female Householders 1970-79, Series P-23, No. 107: Department of Health and Human Services, Administration of Children, Youth and Families, *The Status of Children, Youth and Families*, 1980.
36. Gilder, *Wealth and Poverty*, p. 68.
37. *Ibid.*, p. 115.
38. Frank Ackerman, *Reaganomics: Rhetoric vs Reality* (Boston: South End Press, 1982), p. 29.
39. Nancy Mudrick, "The Use of AFDC by Previously High and Low-Income Households," *Social Service Review*, March 1978.
40. Martin Rein and Lee Rainwater, "Patterns of Welfare Use," *Social Service Review*, December 1978, cited by National Advisory Council Report, p. 21.
41. See Nick Kotz, "The War on the Poor," *The New Republic*, March 24, 1982; Ackerman, *Reaganomics*, p. 30; Sar Levitan, *Programs in Aid of the Poor for the 1980s (Baltimore: The John Hopkins Press, 1980) p. 31, cited by National Advisory Council Report, p. 31. U.S. Department of Health and Human Services, AFDC Recipient Characteristics Study, 1979.*
42. The Bureau of National Affairs, *Employment and Training Reporter*, 13:34, May 5, 1982.
43. Ackerman, *Reaganomics*, pp. 86-87.
44. Ben Bedell, "White House Pushes Workfare Program," *Guardian*, April 28, 1982, p. 3.
45. Bedell, "White House Pushes Workfare Program," p. 3.
46. "States Prove More Enterprising," *Business Week, November 29, 1982, p. 63; New York Times*, October 9, 1982.
46. Robert Greenstein, *The Effect of the Administration's Budget, Tax, and Military Policies on Low Income Americans,"* (Washington, D.C.: Interreligious Taskforce on U.S. Food Policy, February 1983), p. 6, p. 8.
47. Institute for Labor Education and Research, *We Are Not the Problem!*.
48. Greenstein, *The Effect of the Administration's Budget, Tax, and Military Policies*, p. 1.
49. Community Institute Weekly, XII:25 (June 24, 1982), p. 4.
50. *New York Times*, October 6, 1982.
51. Anthony Lewis, *New York Times*, op. ed. January 10, 1983.
52. Greenstein, *The Effect of the Administration's Budget, Tax, and Military Policies*, p. 5.
53. Jobs With Peace, "Your Taxes, Your Choice," Boston, 1983.
54. CBS New, January 20, 1983.
55. Marion Anderson, *Neither Jobs Nor Security: Women's Unemployment and the Pentagon* (Lansing, Michigan: Employment Research Associates, 1980).

56. Frances Fox Piven, "An Agenda for Economic Recovery—Barbara Ehrenreich Interviews Frances Fox Piven," *Ms.*, January 1983, p. 42.
57. Milwaukee County Welfare Rights Organization, *Welfare Mothers Speak Out* (New York: W.W. Norton, 1972), p. 12.
58. Institute for Labor Education and Research, *What's Wrong With the U.S. Economy?*, p. 2.
59. *Ibid.*, pp. 2 and 11.
60. William Tabb, "The Trilateral Imprint on Domestic Economics," in *Trilateralism: The Trilateral Commission and Elite Planning for World Management*, Holly Sklar, ed. (Boston: South End Press, 1980), p. 218.
61. "An Interview with Bennett Harrison and Barry Bluestone," *Working Papers*, January-February 1983, p. 44.
62. Arthur M. Okun, *Equality and Efficiency, The Big Tradeoff*, (Washington, D.C.: The Brookings Institute, 1975).
63. Barbara Kinach et al, "The Effects of Military Spending on Education and the Economy in Massachusetts," a pamphlet by the Jobs With Peace Campaign and the Massachusetts Teachers Association, August 1982.

SELECTED READINGS

Books

Ackerman, Frank. *Reaganomics: Rhetoric vs. Reality*. Boston: South End Press, 1982.

Asian American Studies Center. *Asian Women*. Los Angeles: University of California, 1975.

Bluestone, Barry and Harrison, Bennett. *The Deindustrialization of America: Plant Closings, Community Abandonment, and the Dismantling of Basic Industry*. New York: Basic Books, 1982.

Braverman, Harry. *Labor and Monopoly Capital: The Degradation of Work in the Twentieth Century*. New York: Monthly Review Press, 1974.

Cade, Toni, ed. *The Black Woman: An Anthology*. New York: The New American Library/Mentor Books, 1970.

Davis, Angela. *Women, Race and Class*. New York: Random House, 1981.

Domhoff, G. William. *The Powers That Be: Processes of Ruling Class Domination in America*. New York: Vintage Books, 1979.

Ehrenreich, Barbara. *The Hearts of Men: American Dreams and the Flight From Commitment*. New York: Anchor Press/Doubleday, 1983.

Gartner, Greer and Reissman, eds. *What Reagan Is Doing To Us*. New York: Harper and Row, 1982.

Gordon, Linda. *Woman's Body, Woman's Right: A Social History of Birth Control in America*. New York: Penguin Books, 1974.

Hooks, Bell. *Ain't I a Woman: Black Women and Feminism*. Boston: South End Press, 1981.

Hull, Scott and Smith, eds. *All the Women are White, All the Blacks Are Men, But Some of Us Are Brave: Black Women's Studies*. Old Westbury, New York: The Feminist Press, 1982.

Institute for Labor Education and Research. *What's Wrong With the U.S. Economy? A Popular Guide for the Rest of Us*. Boston: South End Press, 1982.

Joseph, Gloria I. and Lewis, Jill. *Common Differences: Conflicts in Black and White Feminist Perspectives*. New York: Anchor Press/Doubleday, 1981.

Katznelson, Ira and Kesselman, Mark. *The Politics of Power: A Critical Introduction to American Government*. New York: Harcourt Brace Jovanovich, 2nd edition, 1979.

Lerner, Gerda, ed. *Black Women in White America: A Documentary History*. New York: Vintage Books, 1973.

McAdoo, Harriette, ed. *Black Families*. Beverly Hills: Sage Press, 1981.

Moraga, Cherrie and Anzaldua, Gloria, eds. *This Bridge Called My Back: Writings by Radical Women of Color*. Watertown, Massachusetts: Persephone Press, 1981.

Piven, Frances Fox and Cloward, Richard. *The New Class War: Reagan's Attack on the Welfare State and Its Consequences.* New York: Pantheon Books, 1982.

———. *Poor People's Movements: Why They Succeed, How They Fail.* New York: Pantheon Books, 1977.

———. *Regulating the Poor: The Functions of Public Welfare.* New York: Random House, 1971.

Rowbotham, Sheila. *Woman's Consciousness, Man's World.* Baltimore: Penguin Books, 1973.

Schechter, Susan. *Women and Male Violence: The Visions and Struggles of the Battered Women's Movement.* Boston: South End Press, 1982.

Sklar, Holly, ed. *Trilateralism: The Trilateral Commission and Elite Planning for World Management.* Boston: South End Press, 1980.

Tabb, William K. *The Long Default: New York City and the Urban Fiscal Crisis.* New York: Monthly Review Press. 1982.

Other Publications

Bethel, Lorraine and Smith, Barbara, eds. *Conditions Five: The Black Women's Issue.* 1979.

Children's Defense Fund. *A Children's Defense Budget: An Analysis of the President's Budget and Children.* Washington, D.C., 1982.

Cabezas, Amado Y. *The Employment Status of Asian-Pacific Women: A Bibliography.* San Francisco: A.S.I.A.N., 1976.

U.S. Department of Education, National Institute of Education, October 1980. *Conference on the Educational and Occupational Needs of Asian-Pacific-American Women, August 24-25, 1976.*

Eisenstein, Zillah. *"Antifeminism in the Politics and Election of 1980." Feminist Studies* 7:2 (1981).

Fuentes, Annette and Ehrenreich, Barbara. *Women in the Global Factory.* New York/Boston: Institute for New Communications/South End Press, 1983.

Gordon, Linda and Hunter, Allen. "Sex, Family and the New Right: Anti-Feminism as a Political Force." *Radical America.* Winter 1977-78.

Greenstein, Robert with Bickerman, John. *The Effect of the Administration's Budget, Tax, and Military Policies on Low Income Americans.* Washington, D.C.: Interreligious Task Force on U.S. Policy, February 1983.

"Third World Women," *Heresies, A Feminist Publication on Art and Politics.* 2:4 (1979).

Lippin, Tobi, ed. "Working Women." *Southern Exposure* IX:4 (Winter 1981).

National Education Association. *Inequality of Sacrifice: The Impact of the Reagan Budget on Women.* Washington D.C., May 1982.

Petchesky, Rosalind Pollack. "Antiabortion, Antifeminism, and the Rise of the New Right." *Feminist Studies* 7:2 (1981).

Rix, Sara E. and Stone, Anne J. *Impact on Women of the Administration's Proposed Budget.* Washington, D.C.: Women's Research and Educational Institute/Congressional Caucus for Women's Issues, April 1982.

Women for Economic Justice. *Poverty Has a Feminine Face.* Boston: forthcoming, 1983.

■RESOURCE ORGANIZATIONS■

Alliance Against Sexual Coercion
P.O. Box 11
Cambridge, MA 02139

Asian Women United
3538 Telegraph Street
Oakland, CA 94609

ter on Budget and Policy Priorities
Massachusetts Avenue, N.E.
shington, D.C. 20002

ter for Constitutional Rights
Broadway
 York, NY 10003

ldren's Defense Fund
C Street, N.W., Suite 400
shington, D.C. 20001

alition of Labor Union Women (CLUW)
Union Square
 York, NY 10003
l free: (800) 221-1930

alition for Reproductive Rights of Workers
6 16th Street, N.W.
shington, D.C. 20036

ta Center (*New Right Monitor*)
 19th Street
kland, CA 94612

splaced Homemakers Center
tional Puerto Rican Forum
15 Crescent Street
ng Island City, NY 11100

splaced Homemakers Network
5 Eighth St., N.W.
ashington, D.C. 20001

strict 925, Service Employees International
 Union (SEIU)
llective Bargaining and Representation
 for Clerical Workers
ll free: (800) 424-2936

od and Hunger Hotline
 Murray Street, Fifth Floor
 w York, NY 10007

od Research and Action Center
19 F Street, N.W.
ashington, D.C. 20004

ray Panthers
35 Chestnut Street
iladelphia, PA 19104

stitute for Labor Education and Research
53 Broadway, Room 2014
 w York, NY 10003

idwest Research, Inc.
 search about the Right)
3 S. Dearborn Street, Suite 1505
icago, IL 60604

Migrant Legal Action Program
806 15th Street, N.W.
Washington, D.C. 20005

National Coalition Against Domestic Violence
P.O. Box 31015
Santa Barbara, CA 93105

National Coalition Against Sexual Assault
Kathy Adams House
54 1/2 Broad Street
Charleston, SC 29401

National Congress of Neighborhood Women
249 Manhattan Avenue
Brooklyn, NY 11211

National Council of La Raza
1725 I Street, N.W.
Washington, D.C. 20006

National Gay Task Force
80 5th Avenue, Suite 1601
New York, NY 10011

National Hispanic Women's Network
150 Columbia Heights
Brooklyn, NY 11201

National Institute for Women of Color
1712 N Street, N.W.
Washington, D.C. 20036

National Organization for Women (NOW)
425 13th Street, N.W.
Washington, D.C. 20004

Nationwide Women's Program
American Friends Service Committee
1501 Cherry Street
Philadelphia, PA 11902

NOW Legal Defense and Education Fund
132 W. 43rd Street
New York, NY 10036

National Women's Health Network
224 7th Street, S.E.
Washington, D.C. 20003

Older Women's League
P.O. Box 11450
Washington, D.C. 20008

Organization of Pan Asian American Women
915 15th Street, N.W., Suite 600
Washington, D.C. 20005

Redistribute Ame...
1 Union Square, ...
New York, NY 1000...

Reproductive Right...
17 Murray Street, Fi...
New York, NY 10007

Rural American Wom...
1522 K Street, N.W.
Washington, D.C. 2000...

Sisterhood of Black Singl...
1360 Fulton Street
Brooklyn, NY 11217

Southeast Women's Employ...
33 Route 5
Versailles, KY 40383

Southerners for Economic Just...
P.O. Box 240
Durham, NC 27702

Women for Economic Justice
145 Tremont Street, Room 607
Boston MA 02111

Women in the Eighties Project
Center for Investigative Reporting
54 Mint Street, Fourth Floor
San Francisco, CA 94103

Lisa Carlson	March 1982	Marcy May	January
Brenda C.	October 1982	Harriette McAdoo	February
Elizabeth C.	November 1982	Onalee McGraw	February
Jean Entine	December 1982	Carol McVicker	February
Estel Fonseca	February 1983	Carol McVicker	January
Theresa Funicello	December 1982	Susan Michaels	February
William Goldsmith	March 1982	Barbara Omolade	January
Carmen Gonzales	February 1982	Avis Parke	February
Bennett Harrison	March 1982	Diana Pearce	February
Sharon Hunt	November 1982	Frances Fox Piven	March
Linda Johnson	January 1983	Anna Lee Saxenian	March
Alan Kahan	January 1983	Susan Schechter	December
Donna Lawrence	November 1982	William Tabb	April
Donna Lawrence	January 1983	William Tabb	December
Connie Marshner	March 1982	Kathleen Teague	February
Khadijah Matin	January 1983		

* Some of these interviews were conducted initially for "The Nouveau Poor," *Ms.*, J...
/August 1982.